D0754723

NO LONGER PROPERTY OF
KING COUNTY LIBRARY SYSTEM

KIRKLAND LIBRARY

OCT   2009

A Robbie Reader

Meet Our New Student From

MALI

KING COUNTY LIBRARY SYSTEM, WA

Oludamini Ogunnaike

P.O. Box 196
Hockessin, Delaware 19707
Visit us on the web: www.mitchelllane.com
Comments? email us: mitchelllane@mitchelllane.com

Mitchell Lane
PUBLISHERS

Meet Our New Student From

Australia • China • Colombia • Great Britain
• Haiti • India • Israel • Japan • Korea • Malaysia •
Mali • Mexico • New Zealand • Nicaragua • Nigeria
• Quebec • South Africa • Tanzania • Zambia •
Going to School Around the World

Copyright © 2010 by Mitchell Lane Publishers

All rights reserved. No part of this book may be reproduced without written permission from the publisher. Printed and bound in the United States of America.

PUBLISHER'S NOTE: The facts on which the story in this book is based have been thoroughly researched. Documentation of such research can be found on page 44. While every possible effort has been made to ensure accuracy, the publisher will not assume liability for damages caused by inaccuracies in the data, and makes no warranty on the accuracy of the information contained herein.

To reflect current usage, we have chosen to use the secular era designations BCE ("before the common era") and CE ("of the common era") instead of the traditional designations BC ("before Christ") and AD (anno Domini, "in the year of the Lord").

**Library of Congress
Cataloging-in-Publication Data**

Ogunnaike, Oludamini.
  Meet our new student from Mali / by Oludamini Ogunnaike.
     p. cm. — (Robbie reader, meet our new student from)
  Includes bibliographical references and index.
  ISBN 978-1-58415-734-2 (library bound : alk. paper)
  1. Mali—Juvenile literature. I. Title.
  DT551.22.O387 2010
  966.23—dc22
                                          2009001123

Printing 1 2 3 4 5 6 7 8 9

                                          PLB

CONTENTS

Mali

Bamako, the capital of Mali, as seen from the old bridge. The president's mansion sits on top of the hill, and between the roads stands a monument to the numerous students killed in demonstrations against Moussa Traoré's regime in 1991.

A New Classmate

Chapter

David couldn't wait to get to school. He jumped off the bus and hustled through the hallways to his third-grade classroom. "Did she come yet?" David panted.

"Oh my, David. Please catch your breath and calm down," Mrs. Patterson said. "Our new student won't be arriving until next Tuesday." Seeing David's face fall, the teacher quickly added, "But don't worry, I've decided that we can spend the day learning about her country, Mali, so that we'll be ready when she comes next week." David smiled again. Yesterday, Mrs. Patterson had told the class that a new student was coming to join their class from Africa, and David was eager to meet her.

Even though Grandma Esther had told him that their ancestors had come from Africa a long, long time ago, David had never met anyone who lived in Africa. He was full of questions. What did people eat there? What did their houses look like? Were

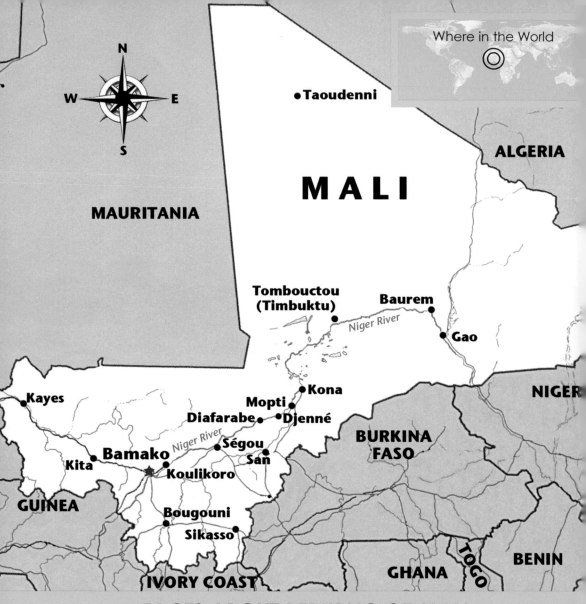

•Taoudenni

ALGERIA

MALI

MAURITANIA

Tombouctou
(Timbuktu)

Baurem

Niger River

•Gao

Kona

NIGER

Kayes

Mopti

Diafarabe

Djenné

Ségou

BURKINA
FASO

Bamako

Niger River

San

Kita

Koulikoro

GUINEA

Bougouni

Sikasso

TOGO

BENIN

GHANA

IVORY COAST

FACTS ABOUT REPUBLIC OF MALI

Mali Total Area:
770,000 square miles
(1.24 million square kilometers)

Population:
12,324,029 (July 2008 estimate)

Capital City:
Bamako

Monetary Unit:
Communauté Financière Africaine
franc

Religions:
Islam, indigenous beliefs, Christianity

Ethnic Groups:
Mande (Bambara, Malinke, Soninke),
Fulani, Voltaic (Dogon, Senufo, Bobo),
Songhai, Tuareg, and Moor

Languages:
French (official), Bamana (Bambara),
Pulaar, Songhai, and several others

Chief Exports:
Cotton, gold, livestock

fun FACTS

Some of the major peoples in Mali are the Bambara, Fulani, Soninke, Songhai, and Dogon. The largest tribe is the Bambara, many of whom work as civil servants. It is the Dogons and the Tuareg who practice a more traditional way of life.

there lions and giraffes and elephants running around like on TV? What kind of TV shows did people watch in Mali?

"Good morning, class!" said Mrs. Patterson.

"Good morning, Mrs. Patterson!" the class replied.

"As many of you know, our new student from Mali will be joining our class next week. In preparation for her arrival, today we will be learning all about her home country. Can anyone find Mali on the map?"

David raised his hand. He had found Mali on the globe in his bedroom the night before.

"Yes, David?" Mrs. Patterson called out. "Come on up to the world map."

David excitedly pointed to a big country in the middle of West Africa. He thought Mali was shaped funny, like a butterfly or a sailboat.

"Very good," Mrs. Patterson said. "The name of the country comes from the word for hippopotamus in Bamana, the main language of the country," she

continued. "While you're up here, can you find the capital for us?"

David scanned the map and then pointed to a little star in southern Mali. The name next to the star was Bamako (BAH-mah-koh). "Well done, David.

A child straps wood and straw to a donkey. Donkeys, or *faliw* in Bamana, are very important for labor in rural areas of Mali.

Class, our new student is from Bamako, the capital city of Mali."

"Mrs. Patterson, what is our new student's name?"

"Her name is Fatou."

Some of the kids in the class giggled. "Does that mean she's fat?" one of them asked.

"No, Brandon, that doesn't mean she's fat. I'm sure some of our names will sound funny in Fatou's language, too."

"Wait, she doesn't speak English? What language does she speak?" Brandon interrupted.

"What kind of food does she like to eat?" Stephanie asked from the back of the room.

"One at a time, class. We'll have to ask Fatou what kind of food she likes to eat when she comes. And yes, she does speak some English, but she has grown up speaking Bamana at home and French at school," Mrs. Patterson answered.

She must be really smart to speak three languages, David thought. *I can't wait to meet her!*

Mali

Mansa Musa (on the black horse) prepares to leave on his holy journey, the Hajj, as painted by Alphonse Etienne Dinet.

Empires, Kings, and Gold

Chapter  2

A long, long time ago, the part of West Africa that we call Mali was home to many great empires and kingdoms. The first major civilization that we know of in this region was called Ghana, which means "warrior king." Between 300 and 500 CE, the people of Ghana became rich and powerful mining gold, farming, trading, and making a strong army with new weapons. But around the year 1200, there was a **drought**, and food became scarce. At the same time, the people surrounding the kingdom attacked it to capture its gold mines. The mighty kingdom of Ghana faded away.

At that time, a new empire, called Mali, was beginning to the east of Ghana. Before it became a great empire, Mali was just a small kingdom of the Mande people. The "Lion King," Sundiata, changed this kingdom into one of the greatest empires in Africa. **Djelis,** or professional musicians, in Mali still tell his remarkable story.

Sundiata

Sundiata was the son of a mighty king, but as a young child he could not speak or walk. After his father died, his brother took over and made life very hard for Sundiata and his mother. Sundiata surprised everyone one day by forcing himself to start walking with the help of an iron rod.

Fearing for his safety, Sundiata went into exile. He traveled from village to village with his mother, until they reached Mema. There, the king took him in and raised him as his own son.

After many years, Sundiata was summoned to return to his home, because the sorcerer-king Sumanguru had conquered his homeland. Sundiata gathered a great army of friends and allies and led them to Kirina, where they fought Sumanguru. Sundiata had learned Sumanguru's weakness, and during the battle, he shot the sorcerer-king with an arrow tipped with the spur of a white rooster. Even though the arrow only grazed Sumanguru's shoulder, the magic arrow defeated him, and he fled with his army.

Sundiata reclaimed his father's throne and built an empire that included all the lands of his allies and his defeated enemy. The name of this empire was Mali.

One of Sundiata's descendants, Mansa Musa, became Mali's greatest ruler. He expanded the empire until it became almost as big as the **continent**

of Europe. Mansa Musa created trade routes across the Sahara, built many beautiful **mosques,** and captured the important city of Timbuktu. Its universities became some of the best in the world. But Mansa Musa is most famous for his **hajj,** or pilgrimage (PIL-grih-midj), to the holy city of Mecca. Like the rest of

The mud mosque of Djenné is the largest mud-block building in the world. It was originally built in the thirteenth century, but fell into disrepair. It was rebuilt once in 1836 and again 1906.

the Mande kings, Mansa Musa was a **Muslim**. The religion of **Islam** requires its followers, called Muslims, to travel to Mecca at least once in their lives if they are able.

When Mansa Musa went on his hajj in 1324, he brought several thousand people and several thousand pounds of gold. Along his journey, he gave away the gold. In fact, he gave away so much gold that the price of gold fell for several years. (Whenever there is too much of anything, it loses its value.) Because of his hajj, people as far away as Europe and Central Asia knew about Mansa Musa, his fabulous wealth, and his great empire of Mali. After Mansa Musa died in 1337, his son Maghan I became mansa (king). He was not a very good ruler, and the once-great empire of Mali fell into decline.

Songhai

While the empire of Mali was crumbling, a new empire was growing to the east. Two princes who had lived in the court of Mansa Musa used what they had learned there to win independence (in-dee-PEN-dents) for their city, Gao. They started a new empire for their people, the Songhai. Years later, in 1464, Sunni Ali Ber took the Songhai throne and became the greatest warrior king since Sundiata.

Sunni Ali Ber captured Timbuktu, the jewel of the Mali empire, in 1468. Then he led his armies down the Niger River, expanding his empire until he

reached the city of Djenné. Djenné is often called Timbuktu's sister city, because both cities were great centers of learning. Unlike Timbuktu, however, Djenné had never been captured by the Mali empire. After trying 99 times, the rulers of Mali finally gave up, and Djenné remained independent until Sunni Ali Ber arrived. The Songhai king and his army surrounded the city, but the people of Djenné did not give up easily. They held off the Songhai army for seven years, seven months, and seven days. Weakened by **famine**, they surrendered in 1473. This victory established the Songhai Empire as the new power in West Africa.

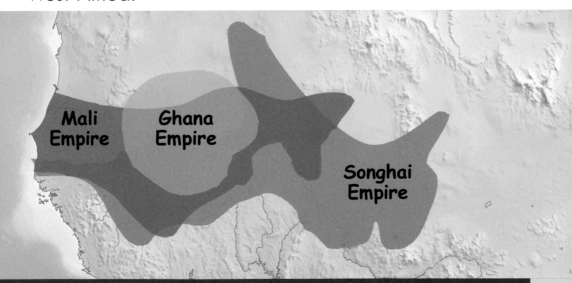

Mali Empire

Ghana Empire

Songhai Empire

The empires of Ghana, Mali, and Songhai succeeded each other in ruling over what is today the country of Mali, and many other countries in West Africa as well. At its peak, the Songhai empire stretched over 800,000 square miles, an area roughly the size of Western Europe (France is around 221,000 square miles in area).

fun FACTS

The Cattle Crossing is an important Fulani festival. Every December, herders bring their cattle to the river at Diafarabe. The herders meet their families on the other side of the river for the festival. There is a competition to judge the fattest and best cared for cattle. The winner gets a robe or blanket. The loser gets a peanut. When the festival is over, the herders take the cattle to new pastures.

One of Sunni Ali Ber's generals, Askia Muhammad Touré, seized the throne in 1493. Touré expanded his empire west to the Atlantic Ocean and east to the Hausa kingdoms of what is now Nigeria. During Touré's rule, the universities of Timbuktu drew scholars from around the world, who wrote many important books. This time is considered the zenith (ZEE-nith), or peak, of civilization in Western Africa.

This golden age did not last forever. In 1591, the sultan of Morocco sent an army to invade Songhai. Armed with gunpowder rifles, the Moroccan army conquered Gao, Timbuktu, and Djenné. The soldiers carried away many of the empire's nobles and scholars in chains. The empire dissolved into several small kingdoms. In the late 1800s, French armies conquered these kingdoms, uniting them along with most of West Africa into a colony called the French Sudan.

The people of Mali did not like being ruled by France, and after a long struggle, the Republic of

Amadou Toumani Touré, a former general and elected president of Mali, was given the title "soldier of democracy" after he overthrew the military government of Moussa Traoré and handed power over to civilian leadership.

Mali declared independence from France on September 22, 1960. The country was ruled by a military dictatorship from 1968 to 1991, when Amadou Toumani Touré overthrew the military government. Touré, or ATT, was elected president in 2002 and again in 2007.

Mali has become one of the most politically stable countries in Africa, but it remains very poor. Malians have had to struggle with droughts, high unemployment, and corruption in the government.

Mali

Mali's desert elephants migrate almost 300 miles in a year, as far as 35 miles in a day. They travel to find water. They share their territory with the nomadic Tuareg.

The Land of Mali

Chapter **3**

Mali is shaped by three main features: the Sahara in the north; the Niger River, which runs diagonally through the middle of the country; and the forest of the southeast. The Sahara is the largest hot desert in the world. It is bigger than Australia, and almost as big as the United States. The Sahara has been growing larger for the past several hundred years, and in some places it is expanding as fast as 30 miles a year. This spreading of the desert is called **desertification** (deh-zer-tih-fih-KAY-shun). The area around Timbuktu used to have forests, farmlands, and many kinds of wildlife, but these have disappeared as the Sahara has taken over the land.

The people who live in the Sahara desert are mainly **nomadic**. They make their living by herding livestock or trading goods such as salt and silver, which they carry across the desert in **caravans**. The ancient empires of Ghana, Mali, and Songhai grew rich exporting salt and gold to North Africa and Europe, and salt and gold are still two of the country's most important **exports**.

The Niger River starts in the forest highlands just beyond the southeast border of Mali. It cuts all the way up into the Sahara, then turns south and empties into the Gulf of Guinea on the coast of Nigeria. The Niger is Africa's third longest river and provides water,

A sandstorm from the Sahara blasts through Mali. Winds from the Sahara, called harmattan, sweep southward, carrying sand and dust across the dry grasslands of Mali every year.

The Niger River is a major trade route. Merchants and fishermen in dugout canoes with colorful designs travel up and down the river buying and selling their wares at different port cities.

fish, and even electricity (through **hydroelectric** dams) to the people of Mali. The river floods every summer, enriching the soil for farmers. Almost all of Mali's major cities and best farmlands are found close to the Niger.

Timbuktu camel caravan. In the northern deserts of Mali, camels are very important animals. They can carry people and goods across long distances in the desert. Camels can carry up to 900 pounds, and go a very long time without water.

Farmers harvest a Bamako garden. Even in the capital city of Bamako, many people still farm crops such as corn, lettuce, and tomatoes. The farmland depends on water from the Niger River.

The forests of southeast Mali are home to much of the country's wildlife, including elephants and lions. Most of Mali's gold is also found in this region. However, as the Sahara expands, the forest region grows smaller.

The border between the forest and the desert is called the Sahel. In this dry grassland, people herd cattle, hunt, and farm. Lions and elephants still roam the Sahel, and many hippopotamuses and crocodiles live in the Niger River. Not many animals can survive in the desert, but many nomads who live there own herds of camels, sheep, and goats.

Mali

Dogon dancers perform in fancy masks for different rituals such as funerals and initiation ceremonies throughout the year. The masks are passed down from father to son, and some of them are very old, although they are newly decorated each year.

The People and Cultures of Mali

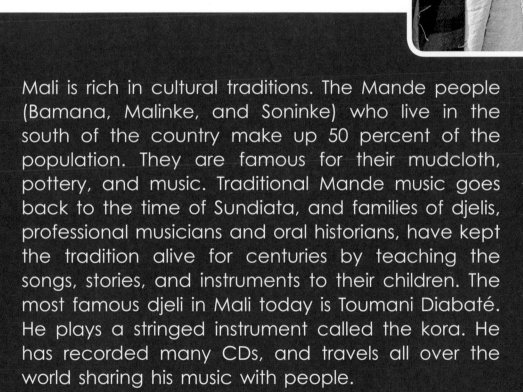

Chapter 4

Mali is rich in cultural traditions. The Mande people (Bamana, Malinke, and Soninke) who live in the south of the country make up 50 percent of the population. They are famous for their mudcloth, pottery, and music. Traditional Mande music goes back to the time of Sundiata, and families of djelis, professional musicians and oral historians, have kept the tradition alive for centuries by teaching the songs, stories, and instruments to their children. The most famous djeli in Mali today is Toumani Diabaté. He plays a stringed instrument called the kora. He has recorded many CDs, and travels all over the world sharing his music with people.

The Fulani people, who make up about 20 percent of the population of Mali, are traditionally nomadic herders. They are famous for their jewelry and blankets. The Dogon people who live in the middle of the country build their homes high in the cliffs. They carve intricate masks which they don and dance with in festivals and rituals such as funerals. The Tamashek, or Tuareg, of the north are known for their silver jewelry, swords, and elaborate turbans.

Each ethnic group has its own festivals and celebrations, but every Sunday in Bamako, where many different people live together, the sound of honking horns and music signal a wedding. One of the highlights of this celebration is when the women,

World-famous kora player and djeli Toumani Diabaté performs with his band. Diabaté is perhaps Mali's most famous musician, and he has used his fame to popularize traditional Malian music abroad while preserving it at home. He founded a musical academy in Bamako where young Malians can study traditional music.

Mudcloth is a Malian specialty. Handwoven cotton is dyed with different types of mud to produce patterns like the one above.

A beaded jacket, hat, and scabbard (sheath for a knife) feature the bold geometrical patterns typical of Mali crafts. These and other beaded items, such as tapestries, are sold as traditional Mali crafts in Mopti and other cities.

all dressed in their best clothes, form a circle and dance as the drummers play rhythms faster and faster. Weddings are usually held out in the open, and attract people from all over the neighborhood. The women of the family work hard making large pots of *zame* (ZAH-may), a special rice dish with meat, to serve the guests.

Bamako is the fastest growing city in Africa. With a population of 1.7 million, it is home to roughly

People returning from a wedding in the village of Noumana. In smaller, rural areas, nearly the entire village participates in weddings, which may take several days and involve lots of drumming and dancing.

14 percent of Mali's 12 million people. Life in the city is very different from life in the villages. Bamako has highways, tall buildings, banks, theaters, a stadium, museums, and a zoo. Most houses in Bamako are made of cement blocks, and many have electricity, running water, and often a television set. Although Bamako has a few supermarkets and stores, most people do their shopping in open-air markets. In most of these markets, there are no fixed prices. People **negotiate** (neh-GOH-shee-ayt) a price that they think is fair. The **currency** in Mali is the CFA franc, which is shared by neighboring Senegal, Côte D'Ivoire (Ivory Coast), Togo, and Benin.

Life in the villages is much quieter and less crowded than in the cities. Many villagers get their water from wells or rivers, and they do not have electricity. Most villagers farm, fish, or raise livestock. They sell fruits and vegetables, such as bananas and onions, in small markets. People from surrounding villages will travel there as well to buy and sell

BCEAO Tower bank, the tallest building in Bamako

their goods. Village houses are usually made from wood, mud, or rock. They are often much cooler in the hot season than the cement houses in the city.

In both village and city life, family is very important, and many Malians live with their extended family in one large house. Most families eat meals together out of the same big platter of food. Most Malian dishes consist of a vegetable or meat sauce served over rice, or with *to* (sounds like "toe"), a paste

Gourds, or calabashes, are very important household items. They are used to store, serve, and carry many types of food and drink. In some areas of Mali, they are even used as musical instruments.

made out of millet. Fried plantains, called *loko* (low-KOW), and french fries are also favorites in the cities. Most Malian dishes are eaten with bare hands. Before and after the meal, everyone washes his or her hands in a bowl of water, starting with the oldest member of the family and ending with the youngest. Malian children are taught to respect their elders, and older people can ask any young person they meet in the street to run an errand for them, such as buying tea from the corner store.

Tea drinking is something of a national pastime in Mali. Many Malian men don't feel fully awake in the morning if they have not had their tea (like many American adults and their coffee). Malian tea is always made in a small pot over coals. In a typical tea ceremony, there are three rounds of tea. The first cup is "bitter as death." The second, sweeter cup is "moderate as life." And the sugary third cup is "as sweet as love." People almost never drink tea alone. Like many other parts of life in Mali, tea drinking is **communal**—that is, people do it together and share with one another.

Soccer is another favorite Malian pastime. From Timbuktu to Bamako, you can find children and young adults playing soccer in the streets. Mali has a good national soccer team with international stars

The green tea that is most popular in Mali originally came from China. It was introduced to West Africa in the late eighteenth century by European traders.

such as Frédéric Kanouté and Mahamadou Diarra.

In Mali, Muslim holidays such as **Eid al-Fitr** (a big feast that marks the end of **Ramadan**, the Muslim month of fasting) and Christian holidays such as Christmas are celebrated by everyone. Ninety percent of Malians are Muslim, 9 percent practice traditional African religions, and around 1 percent are Christian. Despite their differences, Malians of different religions generally get along very well.

Schools in Mali are free, and students between the ages of seven and sixteen are required to go. However, less than half of Mali's children finish primary school, usually because they cannot afford the cost of uniforms, books, and other school fees. Many wealthy Malians send their children

Because of shortages of classroom space and teachers, students of different grade levels may share the same classroom and teacher in public schools in Mali. The schools also do not have as much money as American or European schools, but are otherwise very similar. The government of Mali has encouraged and increased the number of children enrolled in school, but is now struggling to find space for all the new students.

to private schools. Some Malians also send their children to Muslim schools called **madrasas**, where they memorize the Qur'an (kuh-RAN), the holy book of Islam, and learn to read and write in Arabic.

Mali

Fatou was excited to go to school in a new country. She hoped she would be able to make new friends in Delaware.

I Bisimilla, Fatou!

Chapter **5**

The students had been practicing how to greet Fatou in Bamana. A few minutes after the bell rang, there was a knock at the door and Mr. Hamilton, the principal, walked into the classroom with a smiling little girl. "*I Bisimilla*, Fatou!" The class shouted in unison.

Fatou's smile grew wider. "Wow, thank you very much. Who taught you how to welcome me in my language? Is that **bene** over there in the bowl? That is my favorite snack!"

"Do you recognize the music, Fatou?" David asked.

"Yes! That's Toumani Diabaté! This is really wonderful, *Aw ni ce* [OW nee chay], thank you, everybody!"

"Fatou, did you have a TV at your house in Mali?" David's friend Brandon asked.

"Of course," Fatou replied. "My favorite channel was ORTM. It's the Malian national channel, kind of

Fatou is cracking open coconuts after a strong wind blew them out of the tree in her backyard. Many of the larger houses in Bamako have yards enclosed in a compound that often have banana, mango, or other kinds of trees.

ENGLISH	BAMANA
Welcome	*I Bisimilla*
Good morning	*I ni sogoma (ih-NEE soh-GOH-mah)*
Goodbye	*K'an ben (KAHN-ben)*
Thank you	*I ni ce (ih NEE chay)*
Yes	*Owo (aw-WOH)*
No	*Ayi (AI-ee)*

like PBS here. They have lots of cool programs about Malian culture and history. But I always liked watching the American movies on the French channel. Oh yeah, and I love the Jack Bauer show, I think it's called 24 here."

"Really?" asked Brandon. "My mom won't let me watch that one. It's on too late here, and she says I have to be a teenager to see it."

The whole class crowded around Fatou. They had so many questions for her! She showed them some pictures of her home in Bamako. Two of the pictures were of Fatou preparing food.

"Are those onions you're peeling with your sisters?" Stephanie asked.

"No," said Fatou. "They're coconuts, and you really can't peel them. First we crack them over a bowl to catch the coconut milk, then we scrape the soft white insides out of the hard shell."

"Do you use them to make coconut cream pie?" Brandon asked.

Fatou is pounding peppers and onions with a mortar and pestle in the backyard to help her mother make zame (a kind of spicy tomato rice) for dinner. Girls in Mali often help their mothers with household chores such as cooking and washing clothes.

Fatou smiled. "I've never had that, but it sounds good! We eat the white part of the coconut fresh, or sometimes we dry it and eat it like candy. Some people use the milk to make stews, but I like to drink it straight from the coconut!"

"Fatou, why did you leave Mali?" David asked.

After finishing their chores, Fatou and her sisters enjoy a game of ludo, which is similar to the American game Parcheesi. Board games are a popular pastime in Mali.

Football, or soccer, is the most popular sport in Mali, and children and teenagers can be found playing soccer nearly every day in nearly every city and village of the country. Mali is also home to several international soccer stars.

"My dad got a job at a bank here, and he's been living in Delaware for the past few months getting things ready for us."

Just then, the bell for recess rang. "Do you have a basketball hoop on the playground?" Fatou asked David as the students lined up to go outside.

"Yeah, we do. Do you like to play basketball?" David asked.

"I love it, it's my favorite sport! Most of my friends like soccer, but I love basketball!"

"Me too!" David said.

After recess, David invited Fatou to come to his house to shoot some hoops and meet his family. He was excited to introduce them to his new friend from Mali.

How To Make
Bene
(Sesame Seed Honey Sticks)

Things You Will Need

An adult

Measuring cup

Measuring spoon

Spoon for stirring

Tableknife

Frying pan

Pot

Oven mitt

Flat pan, like a cookie sheet

Ingredients

4 ounces sesame seeds

4 tablespoons margarine

1 cup honey

Extra sesame seeds, if desired

Instructions

1. With the help of an adult, heat the sesame seeds in a frying pan (do not use oil) until they begin to jump around and turn golden. Have the adult, using an oven mitt, shake the pan so that the seeds do not stick or burn.
2. Remove the pan from heat and allow the seeds to cool.
3. Again with the adult, melt the margarine in a different, heavy pot, then add honey.
4. Stir continuously until the mixture begins to turn thick and brown.
5. Pour the sesame seeds into the mixture and stir well.
6. Pour the mixture onto a cool, flat pan, such as a cookie sheet.
7. As the mixture cools, cut it into bars or sticks. Coat them with more sesame seeds, if desired.

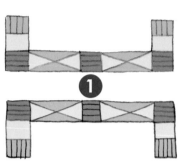

Make Your Own
Kanaga Mask

1

2

3

You Will Need

Yardstick

Stapler

String

Glue

Paint and paintbrushes

Pencil

Scissors

Cardboard

Measuring tape

Markers

The Kanaga mask, carved by the Dogon people, is worn during the Dama ceremony, which is part of the elaborate Dogon funeral rites. The Kanaga mask is said to be a symbol of humankind as the axis of the world, connecting heaven and earth. In modern times, the Kanaga mask has become an emblem of the Dogon people and of Mali itself.

Instructions for a Kanaga Mask

1 With a yardstick or measuring tape and pencil, draw two bracket shapes onto some stiff cardboard, as shown in the drawing. Each should be about 14 inches wide and 7 inches tall.

2 Draw a narrow rectangle on cardboard as well. It should be 17 inches tall and $2^1/2$ inches wide. Cut a small square out of one end to make a "fork." The fork will be the top of this piece.

3 To make the part that goes over your face, fold an $8^1/2$ x 11-inch sheet of paper in half lengthwise. Cut a gentle curve, as shown, along the top corners. Cut a quarter-inch hole through both layers about midway down the outside edge. Cut eye holes and a mouth. Unfold the paper. Trace the design onto cardboard and cut it out.

4 Use glue to attach the two bracket shapes to the long rectangle. The brackets should face in opposite directions to look like the legs of a reptile.

5 Glue the curved top of the face piece to the bottom of the long piece of cardboard. Be sure the fork of the rectangle will be pointing up. You can also reinforce your mask by stapling it. Allow the glue to dry.

6 Use paint or markers to decorate your mask.

7 Tie two pieces of string to the holes on the side of the mask. Tie the string behind your ears and dance!

Further Reading

Books
Burns, Khephra. *Mansa Musa*. New York: Gulliver Books, 2001.
Goss, Linda. *Exploring Mali: A Young Person's Guide to Ancient Civilization*. Norfolk, Virginia: Maya Publications, 2006.
Hirtle, Sheila, and Marq de Villiers. *Timbuktu: The Sahara's Fabled City of Gold*. New York: Walker and Company, 2007.
Van Beek, W.A.E. *Dogon: Africa's People of the Cliffs*. New York: Harry N. Abrams, 2001.

Works Consulted
This book is based on the author's scholarship in African Studies and Religion and on the year he spent living in Mali on a Rockefeller Fellowship. Other sources he used are listed below.

Chu, Daniel, and Eliot Sinnker. *A Glorious Age in Africa: The Story of Three Great Empires*. Trenton: Africa World Press, 2000.
Diouf, Sylviane. *Kings and Queens of West Africa*. New York: Franklin Watts, 2000.
"D'un empire a une republique." Au Coeur du Mali. http://www.geocities.com/infomali/Histoire/intro.htm
Holloway, Kris. *Monique and the Mango Rains: Two Years with a Midwife in Mali*. Long Grove, Illinois: Waveland Press, 2006.
Lucke, Lewis. *Waiting for Rain: Life and Development in Mali, West Africa*. Boston: The Christopher Publishing House, 1998.
Massoff, Joy. *Mali, Land of Gold and Glory*. Waccabuc, New York: Five Pounds Press, 2003.
Wisniewski, David. *Sundiata: Lion King of Mali*. New York: Clarion Books, 1992.

On the Internet
CIA World Factbook
    https://www.cia.gov/library/publications/the-world-factbook/geos/ml.html
Discovering Mudcloth
    http://www.mnh.si.edu/africanvoices/mudcloth/index_flash.html
Mali Country Profile. Library of Congress Federal Research Division
    http://lcweb2.loc.gov

Further Reading

Official Portal of the Government of Mali (in French)
http://www.primature.gov.ml/
Rootsy Records—Great resource on Malian music, particularly
djembe drumming http://www.rootsyrecords.com

Embassy Info
The Embassy of Mali
2130 R Street NW
Washington, D.C. 20008
Phone: 202-332-2249
Fax: 202-332-6603
E-mail: infos@maliembassy.us
URL: http://www.maliembassy.us/new_site/index.htm

Malian Communauté Financière Africaine (CFA) 1000 franc—front (left); back (below)

Malian CFA 10 franc (above)

PHOTO CREDITS: Cover, pp. 8, 9, 21, 22, 24, 25, 27 (bottom), 30, 32, 33—David Rich; pp. 2–3, 19, 27 (top), 28, 34, 35, 36, 38, 39, 48—Oludamini Ogunnaike; p. 4—Robin Taylor/cc-by-2.0; p. 5—Ferdinand Reus/cc-by-sa-2.0; pp. 6, 15—Sharon Beck; pp. 1, 10, 11, —JupiterImages; p. 13—Andy Gillham/GFDL; p. 20—www.carboafrica.net; p. 26—Attila Kisbenedek/AFP/Getty Images; p. 40—Jelle Jansen/cc-by-2.0; p. 42—Joe Rasemas. Every effort has been made to locate all copyright holders of material used in this book. If any errors or omissions have occurred, corrections will be made in future editions of the book.

Glossary

caravan (KAYR-uh-van)—A group of vehicles or animals carrying goods and traveling together over a long distance.

communal (kuh-MYOO-nul)—Shared, or done together.

continent (KON-tih-nent)—One of the large landmasses on Earth.

currency (KUR-un-see)—Something used as money.

desertification (deh-zer-tih-fih-KAY-shun)—The process of land that was fertile changing into a desert.

djeli (JEE-lee)—One of the traditional musicians and historians of Mali.

drought (DROWT)—A long time with no rain.

Eid al-Fitr (EED al-FY-ter)—A Muslim holiday marking the end of Ramadan.

export—A product that a country or company sells to other countries.

hajj (HAHJ)—The pilgrimage to Mecca, the holy city of Islam, that all Muslims are required to make if they are able.

hydroelectric (hy-droh-ee-LEK-trik)—Electricity made from the energy in water.

Islam (IS-lahm)—The religion founded by a prophet named Muhammad in seventh-century Arabia. Islam teaches that God is one and that Muhammad was a prophet of the one God.

madrasa (mahd-RAH-sah)—A Muslim school where children learn the Qur'an and the Arabic language.

mosque (MOSK)—A Muslim place of worship.

Muslim (MUZ-lim)—A follower of the religion of Islam.

negotiate (neh-GOH-shee-ayt)—To bargain or discuss in order to reach an agreement.

nomadic (noh-MAD-ik)—Moving from place to place; not having a permanent home.

Qur'an (kuh-RAN)—The holy book of Islam.

Ramadan (RAH-mah-dahn)—A holy month in the Islamic calendar during which Muslims do not eat between sunrise and sunset.

Index

ABOUT THE AUTHOR

Oludamini Ogunnaike is a PhD student in African Studies and Religion at Harvard University. He spent a year living in Mali on a Rockefeller Fellowship (2007–2008). While in Mali, he studied djembe and kora in Bamako. He also traveled to Timbuktu and Djenné, where he briefly studied medieval political and intellectual history of the region. Mr. Ogunnaike received his bachelor of arts degree in Cognitive Neuroscience and African Studies from Harvard University in 2007. This is his first book.